A souvenir guide

Greys Court

Oxfordshire

C000153473

National Trust

A Peaceful Family Home and Garden

The well-worn fabric of Greys Court hints at its long history – a patchwork of many layers and materials: knapped flint and clay tiles, stone and brick, timber and render. It is a place that reveals itself slowly, as you move through a series of walled courtyards past outbuildings and medieval towers towards the main house. Greys Court may be ancient, but it is not grand.

Above *Prospect of Greys Court*; designed and made in hand-machined fabrics by Lilian Dring, 1964

Making Greys Court

The comfortable family home you see today was created by Sir Felix and Elizabeth, Lady Brunner, who bought the estate in 1937. They restored the house and rescued the garden from dereliction, and here they brought up their four sons.

Sharing Greys Court

The Brunners inherited family traditions of public service: Sir Felix was steeped in Liberal politics and Christian philanthropy; Lady Brunner in the world of the theatre. During the Second World War they welcomed schoolchildren who had been evacuated from London. And when they decided to give the house and garden to the National Trust in 1969, they enthusiastically embraced the opportunity to share with others what they had created at Greys Court. Specially designed new features were added to the garden, and the aroma of boiling jam continued to waft through the house.

The National Trust extends that welcome to everyone, while endeavouring to maintain Greys Court's special sense of peace.

Taking the stage

In the long story of Greys Court, many other characters have walk-on parts: from an archbishop of Canterbury to the drunken 'monks' of the Hell-fire Club; from a beautiful 17th-century poisoner to Jekyll and Hyde; from Peter Pan to the creator of James Bond. You can find them all here.

Right The fireplace in Lady Brunner's Bedroom

A place of peace
'We hope that Greys Court will continue as a place that is helpful not only to enthusiastic archaeologists and gardeners, but also as a haven of peace and quietness for those in need; somewhere where children can enjoy hide-and-seek and the maze, and families can rest for a moment together, away from the pressures of present-day living and find comfort from anxieties.'

Elizabeth Brunner

Key dates

1086
First mentioned in the Domesday book

1346
The De Greys granted 'licence to crenellate' (permission to fortify) Greys Court

1575–6
Sir Francis Knollys rebuilds the main house

1724
Estate passed through marriage to Sir William Stapleton

1758–60s
Sir Thomas Stapleton remodels the house with new plasterwork

1934–7
Mrs Evelyn Fleming briefly owns Greys Court and makes numerous changes

1937
The Brunners buy Greys Court and begin restoring it

1969
The Brunners give Greys Court to the National Trust

Growing up at Greys Court

by Barnabas and Hugo Brunner

We arrived as small boys, four of us aged between ten and two, in this beautiful place on 28 August 1937. Two years later, the Second World War broke out, but it didn't disturb us boys. Nor did it separate our parents: our father, who had served as an artillery officer on the western front in the First World War, was too old for the army. He worked for the Air Ministry and served in the Rotherfield Greys Home Guard. But, of course, we were aware of the conflict and dressed up in military uniform for war games. Evacuees from west London came to stay, in the care of our mother, in the autumn of 1939. Later in the war RAF Benson and the American military hospital in the neighbouring village of Rotherfield Peppard were befriended by our parents, soldiers camped on the estate from time to time, and both Italian and German prisoners of war worked on it.

In July 1944 a V1 flying bomb appeared in the sky close to our prep school in Maidenhead. Its engine cut out and it fell onto a neighbouring jam factory. The explosion blew out some windows in the school, prompting the authorities to put a note in our Sunday letters home to assure our parents that 'None of us were hurt or frightened'. Early in March 1945, Lieutenant-General Richard Gale, commander of Britain's airborne forces, and his staff came to stay with our parents. In his thank-you letter he sympathetically remarked that 'one knows the difficulties which shortage of servants and rationing produce only too well'. A few days later, he participated, as deputy to the commander of the 18th Airborne Corps, US General Matthew Ridgeway, in the largest airborne operation in history: the Rhine Crossings.

From the age of seven our enjoyment of Greys was confined to the school holidays. But when we were there, we made the most of our good fortune. The lawns and gardens were our playground – and our bicycle track. We played cricket, and other games, inside and outside the house. Later on, the fields and woods were the scene of shooting, and of our first experience of work: harvesting cereals, which involved building stooks, at 9 old pence an hour, and scragging up the young trees which our father had started planting soon after he bought the property.

The village and the town of Henley were important to us too. A twenty-minute walk took us to the parish church, where we worshipped regularly and which houses the grand Knollys monument and several lesser memorials to the Stapleton family. A much shorter walk down the back drive and up Grub Hill led to the village green, where we played cricket.

The place remained home until each of us got married. We were fortunate indeed to be brought up here by loving parents and to have Greys Court as part of our lives and our own families', until our mother died in 2003.

The Approach

At its height in the late Middle Ages, Greys Court comprised a substantial complex of buildings and walled courtyards. Today, you approach the house through the surviving fragments of these.

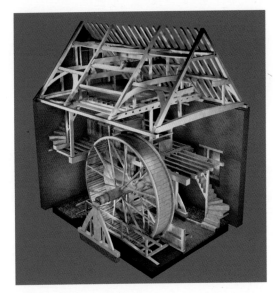

The Dower House

This was probably built in the early 17th century in brick laid in English bond, perhaps by William Knollys. It incorporates the medieval south-east tower. Since the 18th century, it has also been known as the Bachelors' Hall: hence the Latin inscription over the front door '*Melius nil coelebe vita*' ('Nothing is better than the single life'). Until 1939 it was divided into two cottages and in a poor state.

The 'Cromwellian Stables'

It is said to have been used as a mess-room by Cromwellian soldiers who were garrisoning Greys during the Civil War. Dendrochronology (tree-ring analysis) dates its timbers to 1578, and it also has Elizabethan stone fireplaces. It was built as lodgings rather than stables, although it may have been used as such from the mid-17th century, when it was much reduced in length.

The spiral staircase was inserted in the 1930s by Mrs Fleming, based on a historic example in the Victoria & Albert Museum. The salvaged 17th-century panelling was put up at the same time.

The Well House

It was built in 1586–7 over a 200-foot-deep medieval well. Water was raised by a vertical tread-wheel, which was turned by a donkey. This is a very rare, large and early surviving example of this mechanism, which was constructed only 30 years after it was first illustrated in the 1536 edition of Agricola's *De Re Metallica*.

Nearby is a pump dating from about 1870, which was powered by two horses walking in a circle. It came originally from Shabden Park, near Epsom, and was set up here in 1975.

The Green Court

The Green Court, which today provides a lawned setting for the house, was originally divided by a wall into two elements, the upper and base courts. In dry weather you can see parch marks in the grass that reveal the position of vanished medieval buildings and walls. The Brunner boys used the top lawn for cricket, football and other games.

Opposite **The Great Tower and the 'Cromwellian Stables'**

Left **3D computer-aided-design survey of the tread-wheel mechanism in the Well House**

Below **The Dower House from the Great Tower**

Tour of the House

'Framed like a picture by the rarest and stateliest trees … stands Greys Court … erected amongst the remains of a vast old castellated mansion.'

Mary Russell Mitford, *Recollections of a Literary Life* (1851)

The Exterior

The principal front of the house faces east across the upper part of the Green Court (the Elizabethan upper court). It was built in 1575–6 with three gables over three storeys from flint, brick, dressed stone and materials salvaged from the medieval house. However, its present, attractively varied texture would originally have been hidden under render, which was stripped off in the 1930s. The Victorian ground-floor bay windows and the entrance porch which they flanked have also all gone. Over the centuries, the windows have been changed several times, but the façade now resembles quite closely its original Elizabethan appearance.

The oriel window on the south front with its stone mullions and transoms probably dates from the early 17th century. At the opposite end of the house, the two-storey bay window was added to the north front in the mid-18th century as part of Sir Thomas Stapleton's remodelling of the north end of the house, which included creating the higher-ceilinged Drawing Room.

The National Trust undertook major conservation of both the exterior and interior of the house in 2006–9. This entailed re-roofing and re-servicing the building and improving its environmental performance.

The Entrance Hall

Mrs Fleming removed the Victorian porch in 1935–7, when she also inserted the mullioned windows either side of the entrance door. At the same time, she knocked down the left- and right-hand internal walls to transform the three ground-floor rooms along the west front into a single, long room. The Brunners restored the previous arrangement and commissioned the plasterwork in the corners of the ceiling, which features eagles inspired by those in Lady Brunner's Bedroom.

Furniture

The oak-framed *table* in the centre of the room was made in Switzerland for a namesake of Sir Felix, whose family came from that country. The German inscription translates: 'Felix Brunner had me made in the year 1584 in this house I must stay'. It was bought for Sir Felix's grandfather by the British Consul in Zurich in the 1870s. Such tables were designed for playing cards, with the scores being chalked up on the slate slab let into the walnut top.

Opposite Greys Court from the north-east

Right The Entrance Hall

Ceramics

The recessed glass cabinets flanking the door to the Inner Hall display an appropriate mixture of English and Swiss china: Chelsea Red Anchor porcelain, *c*.1752–6, including dessert plates with patterns inspired by plants in Sir Hans Sloane's Botanick Garden at Chelsea; and Zurich hard-paste porcelain hot water pot, coffee pot, teapot and cups and saucers, *c*.1765–75. The Swiss plates were collected by Brunner ancestors, the Samson candlestick figures of the seasons by Lady Brunner.

The Dining Room

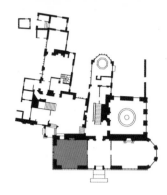

The Brunners used this room for more formal entertaining, but even this was not very formal, with meals being taken at a simple, circular table and Windsor chairs. A jib door to the left of the fireplace connects conveniently with the Kitchen.

This room retains its 16th-century proportions, with the original ceiling height. It would once have been much darker, as there was no window in the east (left-hand) wall until the 19th century, when a bay window was inserted. The Brunners replaced it with the present stone-mullioned window. The 18th-century-style plaster cornice was renovated in the 1940s, with a lion's head motif borrowed from that in the Drawing Room.

The marble chimneypiece is a simpler version of the 1760s pattern in the Drawing Room. It was originally upstairs, but was moved here by Lady Brunner.

Furniture
The Swiss dower *chest*, c.1617, is decorated with the Brunner arms and fountain emblem ('*brunnen*' is German for fountain).

Pictures
Around the room are watercolours by Frank Brangwyn (1867–1956) depicting various scenes throughout Europe, including one inspired by the 1908 earthquake in Messina.

Theatrical memorabilia
The glazed case above the far window contains two belts with daggers and scabbards, which were worn in a production of *Macbeth* by the great Victorian actor-manager Sir Henry Irving, who was Lady Brunner's grandfather.

Opposite The Dining Room

Below *The Messina earthquake*; watercolour by Sir Frank Brangwyn

The Drawing Room
The Inner Hall

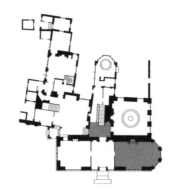

The Drawing Room

In 1758–9 Sir Thomas Stapleton raised the ceiling from its Elizabethan height and added the bow window to create this airy and welcoming room, which enjoys superb views over the garden.

Plasterwork

The ceiling plasterwork is a very fine example of Rococo naturalism. The imagery – courting doves, and bows and arrows – all suggests the theme of love, and so may have been commissioned to celebrate Sir Thomas Stapleton's marriage to Mary Fane in 1765. The craftsman responsible is not known, but may have been a plasterer named Swan, who did similar work at nearby Watlington Park. The 18th-century chimneypiece is made from yellow, black and white marble.

Pictures

The view of Greys Court over the fireplace was painted in egg tempera by James Lynch in 1993, having been commissioned by Lady Brunner through the Maas Gallery.

Sculpture

Bust of Lady Brunner's grandfather, the great Victorian actor-manager Sir Henry Irving.

Furniture

The *chairs* were embroidered in *petit point* during the Second World War by the Women's Needlework Guild. They were bought by Lady Brunner in the 1950s. The *grandfather clock* has an eight-day movement made by S. Townson, London, *c.*1710.

Ceramics

Famille verte Chinese export porcelain.

Christmas at Greys Court

Lady Brunner celebrated family Christmases at Greys Court well into her 90s. A little Christmas tree, suitably decorated, stood on the piano in the Drawing Room, and the walls were decked with holly and ivy from the garden. Any Christmas cards featuring robins were placed on the mantelpiece. A Christmas crib was laid out in the Inner Hall. After Christmas lunch, the family moved into the Schoolroom to watch the Queen's Christmas message on TV, and then into the Drawing Room for music on the piano and harp. The afternoon ended with Lady Brunner's Christmas cake, washed down with Keemun China tea from Fortnums.

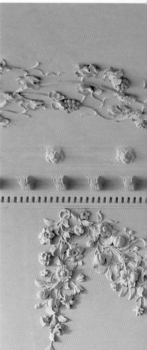

Right above **The Drawing Room**

Right below **Detail of the mid-18th-century plasterwork**

The Inner Hall
Ceramics
The Victorian Staffordshire pottery includes figures of the notorious highwaymen Tom King (shot dead in 1737) and Dick Turpin (hanged in 1739).

Love in old age
The portrait of Sir Felix and Lady Brunner was painted in 1982 by Bill Mundy, a local Henley artist who specialises in painting traditional miniatures. By the time of the commission, Sir Felix was largely confined to bed with Parkinson's, so only the portrait of Lady Brunner was painted from life, but Mundy still managed to achieve a touching image of love in old age.

The Schoolroom

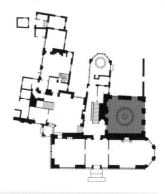

The Schoolroom

This room probably served as the library in the 18th and 19th centuries. The Brunners used it as their dining room until the beginning of the Second World War, when they took in ten children evacuated from London. The young visitors were put up in the nursery. The room served as the schoolroom of the two youngest Brunner boys, who were still living at home. In more recent years, Lady Brunner used the room as her study.

The ceiling was raised in 1758–9, but the plasterwork wreath in the centre of the ceiling seems to have been put up at a later date, as it is distinctly cruder than that in the Drawing Room.

Pictures

Over the fireplace is a portrait of Sir Henry Irving out of costume. On either side of it are paintings by Lady Brunner's brother, the stage designer Laurence Irving. The portrait between the windows is of Sir Felix's grandfather, Sir John Brunner, 1st Bt (1842–1919), the founder of the family fortune. It was painted by Hubert von Herkomer, who began his career painting graphic images of the Victorian poor, but went on to produce more conventional portraits of eminent Victorians such as Sir John. Flanking this portrait are pencil studies of the Brunner boys by David Rolt.

The plaster cast of H.B. Irving's hand was made by the sculptor Paul Raphael Montford and was used in the 1910 stage version of Dr Jekyll and Mr Hyde, in which Lady Brunner's father starred.

Furniture

The oak and fruitwood dower chest is Swiss. Lady Brunner's desk was placed in the corner of the room so that she could enjoy a good view of the arboretum. Her chair is embroidered with a needlework view of Greys Court.

Above right Sir John Brunner, 1st Bt

Below right The Schoolroom

The Staircase
The Landing
The Library

The Staircase

The staircase was altered in 1864–5 and again in the mid-20th century, when the Brunners inserted the mezzanine window.

The Landing

Stained glass

The 16th–17th-century Swiss glass in the window on the landing includes an unusual image of a bakery (1580) and scenes of jousting, fountains and ponds.

The Library

This was Sir Felix's domain, to which he would retire when he wanted quiet. The fireplace was probably created by Mrs Fleming in the 1930s, incorporating a 17th-century wooden overmantel. The Brunners were particularly fond of auriculas – hence the pattern of the curtains.

Books

This is the library of a cultured liberal intellectual who was fond of the Victorian novels of Anthony Trollope. It is also strong in books on politics and gardening, and contains volumes that once belonged to Sir Henry Irving.

Pictures

The view of Greys Court over the fireplace was painted by Lady Brunner's brother, Laurence Irving. It shows the family and staff gardening, painting, playing cricket, walking the dog and gathering flowers for the house.

Double Spare Bedroom
Sir Felix's Bedroom
Lady Brunner's Bedroom

Double Spare Bedroom

Opened to the public for the first time in 2012, this was used as the Brunner's guest bedroom. The door to the left of the bay windows leads into the Dressing Room and the wallpapered door to a small en-suite bathroom. The Maryport curtains are made of screen printed glazed chintz – Maryport was a favourite design of the Queen Mother's and was used to furnish several of her residences.

Sir Felix's Bedroom

The bedrooms are furnished largely as the Brunners had them, with more of their collection of woodcuts by Frank Brangwyn and some fine ceramics.

Lady Brunner's Bedroom

This spacious bedroom may have been a reception room in the 18th century. The mid-18th-century panelling would originally have been painted, but was stripped in the 1930s in the fashion of the time.

Right above Sir Felix's Bedroom

Right below Lady Brunner's Bedroom

The Backstairs
The Kitchen

The Backstairs

These were remodelled by the Brunners in 1940, reusing timbers taken from an earlier, probably 17th-century stair.

The Kitchen

This is both the historic core of the house and the heart of the Brunners' home. Dendrochronology has established that many of the exposed joists and posts survive from the 1450s timber-framed west range, which was buried within later rebuilding. The door to the larder still has its ancient metal lock. The old panelling was discovered in the attic, having probably been discarded during 18th-century changes to the house. When Lady Brunner's Aga had to be replaced in 1987, the old arched fireplace was revealed, and subsequently opened up and repaired.

Picture

The collage of Greys Court was made by Lilian Dring, having been commissioned in 1964 by Lady Brunner, who thought it 'a stupendous job'.

Jam today

Food played a very important part in life at Greys Court. As befitted a former chairman of the National Federation of Women's Institutes, Lady Brunner was an enthusiastic jam and marmalade maker. The aroma of boiling fruit filled the house for much of the summer and autumn.

Below The Kitchen

The Garden

'I remember thinking it marvellous – it was very derelict, the garden especially, but I remember picking up a stone and putting it in my pocket.'

Lady Brunner after her first visit to Greys Court

There is little evidence for the garden before the Brunners arrived in 1937. A grade 2 listed parkland (18th-century) surrounds the garden. Two 18th-century watercolours suggest that the parkland was planted in the informal Picturesque style with Scots pine and other conifers, which could be enjoyed from the bow windows added to the north-east corner of the house in the 1760s.

The garden we see today is very largely a post-war creation of the Brunners. They took as their starting point the views from the house, the Great Tower and the network of ancient walls, enriching the parkland with more trees to north and south of the house, and creating a series of enclosed gardens to the east. While embracing the rich historical resonances of the place, the Brunners created a garden that is at once tranquil and theatrical.

The garden has not stood still since Greys Court was given to the National Trust in 1969; indeed, the pace of change has accelerated. As well as enriching and reviving the planting in accordance with organic principles, the Brunners have commissioned a succession of site-specific garden features and furniture from talented young designers in the Arts and Crafts tradition.

Below Pink aquilegia flowering beside a path in the Rose garden

Opposite
The Great Tower

The Tower Garden

Lady Brunner began laying out this garden in 1938 in the shadow of two of Greys Court's historic towers. She chose a scheme of white-flowering plants: rambling roses, *Magnolia soulangeana*, *Poncirus trifoliata*, jasmine, nicotiana and *Sarcococca confusa*. Lady Brunner's garden has been compared with the famous White Garden at Sissinghurst, but she almost certainly came up with the idea independently. White was in any case a favourite colour in the 1930s.

Work stopped here during the Second World War, but resumed in the 1950s, when Humphrey Waterhouse persuaded Lady Brunner to grub up the Victorian rhododendrons. Beneath the tall Scots pine grow cistus, rosemary, salvias, carpentaria and phlomis.

This tower, my prison

In 1959 and 1961 the Great Tower provided the dramatic backdrop for performances of Robert Gittings's *son et lumière* play, *This tower my prison*, which tells the lurid story of Frances Howard's murder by poisoning of Sir Thomas Overbury in the Tower of London in 1613.

'Peace, a country peace.
Here in the garden at Greys …
Walk free in the formal maze,
Box-hedge, privet and yew,
And camomile under the feet,
All that the gardener grew
Whose nature is known to
   be sweet
Alleys of blossom and scent,
The old walls breathing it back
Render an ancient content.'

Robert Gittings

The Rose Garden
The Wisteria Walk
The Kitchen Garden

The Rose Garden

This garden was designed by Kitty Lloyd Jones, who also worked at Upton (also National Trust), with roses supplied from the Shrewsbury nursery of Hilda Murrell. However, the thin Chilterns soil is not ideal for growing roses, and this garden had to be replanted in 1982 and 2002. On the second occasion, 80 tons of new topsoil and manure were barrowed in by hand.

The garden traces the history of the rose, from the early damask varieties to the modern hybrid perennials. The flanking beds are arranged by colour: oranges and yellows on the north side, pinks and purples on the south. The lilac tree (*Paulownia tomentosa*) is a mass of violet flowers in May.

The oak bench is carved on the front with hedgehogs, flowers and owls by Jacqueline Geldart. It was placed here in 1990 to commemorate Mrs Clemson, who was the Brunners' cook for 42 years from 1938.

The Wisteria Walk

The venerable wisteria was planted around 1890 and, with the bluebells, forms a sea of blue in May. It is underplanted with hellebores, *Iris reticulata* and *Liriope muscari*.

Below *Rosa gallica* 'versicolor' (*Rosa mundi*)

The Kitchen Garden

By the time the Brunners came to Greys
Court in 1937, the Kitchen Garden had been
out of cultivation for 20 years. During the
Second World War, it was brought back
into service to support the 'Dig for Victory'
campaign. The present scheme was first
laid out in 1980 as a traditional *potager*.
The paths are lined with espaliered apple
and pear trees, with 'Ballerina' crab-apples
trained over iron hoops. Redcurrants grow in
the quadrants, while brassicas, alliums and
legumes are planted in rectangular beds at
the north end of the garden. Native bulbs
are planted in two grass areas under the apple
trees forming an early meadow. Peonies are
another particular feature. Four owls carved
by Jacqueline Geldart look down from posts
in the quadrants.

The yew-wood statue at the far end of the
Rosa mundi avenue commemorates Charles
Taylor, who was head gardener at Greys
Court from 1937 to 1955, having served
(like Sir Felix) on the Somme in the First
World War. He was largely responsible for
reviving the derelict garden.

The octagonal stone fountain at the
centre of the garden was designed by Hugo
Brunner's brother-in-law, the architect
Francis Pollen. A prayer for a good harvest
by the Latin poet Horace was carved in slate
by the letter-cutter Michael Harvey, recalling
the probable Roman occupation of the site.

Above The Kitchen Garden
in May

Left The yew-wood statue of
the long-serving Greys Court
gardener Charles Taylor

The Maze
The Cherry Garden
The Knot Garden

The Maze

The brick and turf maze was inspired by Dr Robert Runcie's enthronement address as Archbishop of Canterbury in 1980, in which he spoke of 'the mazelike muddle in which the world finds itself', and his hope that Christian and non-Christian, working together, could solve it. The design, by Adrian Fisher, is packed with Christian symbolism: at the centre are superimposed the Roman and Byzantine crosses, symbolising the western and eastern churches. The seven rings stand for the seven days of creation, the three outward turns for the three days that Christ spent in the tomb. The arms of the Byzantine cross span 33 feet, Christ's age at his crucifixion. Michael Harvey cut the four slate inscriptions, which were drawn from St Augustine, Siegfried Sassoon, Robert Gittings and Julian of Norwich. Archbishop Runcie blessed the maze in October 1981.

The Cherry Garden

Lady Brunner created this garden in 1950 with the advice of the painter and gardener Humphrey Waterfield. Ornamental Japanese cherries and an old tulip tree were set within the walls of the old tithe barn. The cherry trees have gradually succumbed to disease and had to be replaced in 2007. The 18th-century Swiss fountain was added in 1966 as a 40th wedding anniversary present to the Brunners from their children.

The bench was carved with dogs and a wild boar by Jacqueline Geldart and was commissioned in 2004 by the Greys Court volunteers in memory of Lady Brunner, who died in 2003.

The Knot Garden

The Knot Garden is sheltered by the mellow brick walls of the Cromwellian Stables. The beds are laid out as a formal parterre edged with low euonymous hedges. Against the walls grow *Solanum crispum* 'Glasnevin' and pink *Nerene bowdenii*, which is at its best in late autumn. It is enclosed on the south side by a wall of laburnum.

Left The Maze

Right The Knot Garden

Opposite The Ice-house

The Arboretum and Orchard
The Chinese Bridge

Arboretum and Orchard

The garden to the north of the house features many handsome mature trees, including larches, *Catalpa bignonioides* and arbutus, which were suggested by Humphrey Waterfield. The Trust is planting a new orchard nearby, with each tree sponsored by the WI.

The Chinese Bridge

This was designed by Francis Pollen as a Chinese-style 'moon bridge', dedicated to the Brunners' Chinese friend, the cookery writer Dr So Yan-Kit. The area below the bridge is planted with blue irises. The path from the Chinese Bridge leads out of the garden towards the 19th-century ice-house, the thatched roof of which was restored in 1992.

The Families of Greys Court

Greys Court in the 1530s

'3 or 4 very olde towers of stone, a manifest token that it was sume tyme a castle. Ther[e] is a very large courte bui[l]dyd about with tymbar and spacyd with bri[c]ke; but this is of a latter worke.'

John Leland

The De Greys

The earliest surviving fabric above ground is part of a wall connected to the Great Tower, which has been dated to the late 11th or early 12th century. It was constructed by the de Grey family, who had been living at Greys Court since the Domesday Book. In the mid 13th century the estate belonged to Walter de Grey (d.1255), a powerful and wealthy magnate who was also a reforming Archbishop of York. De Grey supported King John, when he was forced to agree to the Magna Carta in 1215 and is named in the charter. He was later Regent of England in Henry III's absence abroad. His grand-nephew, Sir John de Grey (1271–1312), was a professional soldier who was probably responsible for fortifying Greys with substantial masonry curtain walls and towers.

His son, Sir John, the 1st Baron Grey of Rotherfield (1300–59) was also a powerful soldier-knight, fighting in the campaigns of Edward III, who appointed him one of the founding Knights of the Garter and Steward of the Royal Household. On 10 December 1346 he was granted a 'licence to crenellate' Greys, and the major surviving medieval work dates from this period: the Great and North-East Towers and connecting curtain wall, the fortified houses and the upper and lower courts. Robert, 4th Baron Grey (d.1387) was also a soldier, commemorated by a magnificent tomb brass in Rotherfield Greys church, which shows him in armour. On his death in 1387, Greys Court passed to his daughter Joan, who married Lord John Deyncourt, and subsequently to their daughter Alice who married Lord William Lovell (d.1455).

The Lovells

In the early 1450s Alice and William Lovell built a large two-storey, timber-framed wing which projected southward into the lower court. This wing was absorbed within later building work, but fragments of it can still be seen in the Kitchen. Slightly later, a crenellated brick range was constructed on the north side of the lower court; part of which is incorporated in the 'Cromwellian Stables'. Alice died in 1474 leaving Greys Court to her grandson Francis Lovell who was a supporter of the Duke of Gloucester, later Richard III, fighting for him at the Battle of Bosworth in 1485. His estate was confiscated by the Crown and Greys Court given to Jasper Tudor, the new king's uncle. Francis Lovell continued to lead rebellions against Henry VII until he disappeared after fighting on the losing side at Stoke, the last battle of the Wars of the Roses in 1487.

In 1514, Greys Court was granted to Robert Knollys (d.1521), a long-standing member of Henry VII's court. The annual rent was a single red rose, payable at midsummer.

Above Sir John de Grey, one of the original Knights of the Garter

Opposite The Great Tower and curtain walls were built by the de Greys during the 13th and 14th centuries

The Knollyses

Robert Knollys's son, Sir Francis (1511–96), was a devout Protestant, who was forced to spend the years of Mary Tudor's reign abroad. He returned to England on the accession of Queen Elizabeth, who was a cousin of his wife Catherine. Francis was appointed to the Privy Council in 1562 and as MP for Oxford managed the government's business in the Commons. He was also Lord-Lieutenant of the county. In 1568 he was given the highly sensitive job of guarding Mary Queen of Scots. Ten years later, his daughter Lettice was married in secret to the Queen's favourite, Robert Dudley – to Elizabeth's fury.

In the hope that Elizabeth would visit Greys, Sir Francis demolished much of the medieval building and rebuilt it as a fashionable Elizabethan courtier house with the present triple-gabled east façade of knapped flint, brick, stone and render (mostly since stripped off). The work comprised several phases between 1559 and 1596, and also involved remodelling the south front and building the well house and the octagonal south-west tower. But despite all his efforts, the Queen never came.

Sir Francis's funeral in 1596 was a very grand affair, in which his staff as Treasurer of the Royal Household, his helmet, coat and sword, and his Garter insignia were carried in solemn procession to Rotherfield Greys church, where he and his wife are commemorated by recumbent effigies on a massive, canopied tomb. On top of the

Below Sir Francis Knollys the Elder

Left This view of Greys Court probably dates from the mid-18th century. It depicts buildings from the Knollys period

Below Sir Francis Knollys the Younger

tomb kneels an effigy of Knollys's second son and heir, William (*c*.1545–1632), who is thought to have inspired the character of Malvolio in Shakespeare's *Twelfth Night*. William held important positions at the court of James I and was created 1st Earl of Banbury by Charles I. However, the Earl's reputation was badly damaged by the scandalous behaviour of his sister-in-law Lady Frances Howard, who was implicated in the poisoning of Sir Thomas Overbury in 1613 after Overbury had opposed the annulment of her marriage to the 3rd Earl of Essex.

During the early 17th century the south-west wing was added to the Elizabethan house, and the brick Dower House was built. But later generations of the Knollys family seem to have taken less interest in Greys Court (they also owned a large house at Caversham and a mansion in Whitehall). Decline set in during the late 17th century: many buildings on the site were demolished or reduced, including the lodging house
(the so-called Cromwellian Stables), which may have been damaged in the Civil War, when it was occupied by Parliamentarian soldiers. The last in the Knollys line, Lettice Kennedy sold what remained to James Paul in 1688, but continued to live here until her death in 1708.

The Stapletons

Sir William Stapleton, 4th Baronet (1698–1739)

Sir William inherited Greys Court through his marriage to Catherine Paul in 1724, which also brought him Braywick in Berkshire, the principal family seat. His family's wealth came not only from land, but also from sugar plantations in Antigua and Nevis, acquired in the 17th century. But he did not have long to enjoy his good fortune, dying in his early 40s.

Sir Thomas Stapleton, 5th Bt (1727–81)

Sir Thomas succeeded his father at the age of twelve, but did not live at Greys Court (which was let out to the local parson) until after his mother's death in 1753. He enjoyed a thoroughly dissolute youth in the company of his cousin, Sir Francis Dashwood of West Wycombe, as one of the twelve Medmenham Monks who made up the notorious Hell-fire Club. The club may have held meetings in the Dower House, which bears a suitable Latin inscription that translates as: 'Nothing is better than the single life.' Sir Thomas seems to have transformed the surviving fragments of the medieval towers and courtyard walls into Gothick follies as an appropriate setting for the club's cavortings. He certainly added the brick crenellations to the top of the Great Tower.

Sir Thomas renovated the house shortly before his marriage in 1765 to Mary Fane. He added the two-storey bow window to the north front and raised the ceiling of the Drawing Room to accommodate delicate new plasterwork on the theme of romantic love. He also refaced the mid-15th-century timber-framed south-west wing with a Gothick façade in flint (demolished in the 1930s). Mary Stapleton may have been responsible for creating the Gothick dairy, which was more ornamental than practical. All this new work was expensive, and his later years were overshadowed by money worries.

A heavy drinker

'Thomas de Grey [Sir Thomas Stapleton's nickname] and John of Henley consumed four bottles of port, two of claret and one of Lisbon at one sitting.'

Hell-fire Club records for 29 September 1762

Sir Thomas Stapleton, 6th Bt (1766–1831)

In 1788 Sir Thomas inherited the title of Lord Le Despencer and with it the family seat of Mereworth Castle in Kent, which became his primary residence. Greys Court was bought by his widowed mother Mary, who lived on there till 1835. She was followed by her two unmarried daughters, Catherine and Maria, who both lived into their 90s. Catherine did not die until 1863. Like Uppark in West Sussex, Greys Court enjoyed a long period of tranquillity during the first half of the 19th century, when very little was done to the house apart from minor repairs in 1840–1.

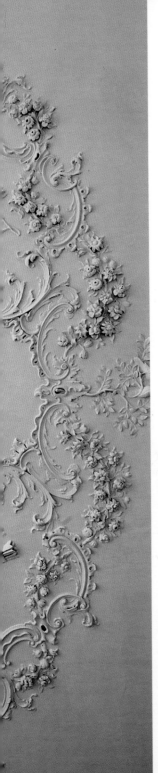

Sir Francis Stapleton, 7th Bt (1807–74)

He was Lord Le Despencer's fourth son, and, like many a younger son, was destined for the church: he served as rector of Mereworth. He certainly did not expect to inherit Greys Court, and when he did so in 1863, he set about repairing the house so that it could be rented out and provide a much-needed income.

Left Sir Thomas Stapleton, 5th Bt, decorated the Drawing Room with fine plasterwork

Below The two-storey bay was added to the north front by Sir Thomas Stapleton, 5th Bt

Sir Francis Stapleton, 8th Bt (1831–99)

He was the first male member of the family to live at Greys Court for almost a century. When he moved in in 1874, he decided to make major changes. He added a billiard room to the north-west wing and a new entrance porch. Between 1883 and 1889 he also added windows to the ground floor of the east front, as well as replacing the small Elizabethan window on the south front. This kind of Victorian embellishment rapidly went out of fashion and none has survived at Greys Court. All that is left from this era is the gate lodge.

Sir Francis had no sons, so the estate and title passed to his nephew, Miles, when he was only six. During the early 20th century the garden was opened to visitors in the summer, but Miles Stapleton seems to have shown little interest in Greys Court, gradually selling off more and more of the estate in the depths of the agricultural depression. The house was finally sold in 1934.

Evelyn Fleming (1934–7)

The Brunners (1937–2003)

The buyer was Mrs Evelyn Fleming, whose late husband, Val Fleming, had been a member of the Scottish banking family and had died in the First World War. Her sons were the creator of James Bond, Ian Fleming, and the travel writer, Peter Fleming. Although the family already owned a large house nearby at Nettlebed, she could not resist buying Greys Court when it came on the market. She lived here for only two years, but in that brief period made substantial and significant alterations. She stripped away the ugly Victorian additions, renovated the antiquated services and created a single 'long room' from the three main reception rooms on the ground floor. She had remodelled her London home on the Chelsea Embankment in a similar way, redecorating the drawing room with gold wallpaper and piles of tomato- and magenta-coloured cushions. However, she does not seem to have had time to apply similar tastes to Greys Court before she sold it in 1937. She had hoped to make it somewhere that her son Peter could write between his travels, but when he married the actress Celia Johnson in December 1935, this plan was abandoned, and with it the house.

The Brunners made further changes in order to create a comfortable family home, but were altogether more sensitive to the historic fabric. They reversed Mrs Fleming's alterations and returned Greys Court to its pre-Victorian state, as well as creating a new garden within the medieval landscape of walls, towers and courtyards. So they restored the arrangement of ground-floor rooms, demolished the kitchen extension and billiard room at the back, built a new kitchen service stair, and inserted more windows on the main stairs. The architect Francis Pollen was commissioned to build a conservatory on the west front in 1984–5. Pollen also designed the Moon Gate Bridge in the garden.

In 1969 the Brunners gave the house, garden and estate to the National Trust, but continued to think of new ways of beautifying Greys Court. They were imaginative patrons of promising young artists and craftsmen, who have filled the house and garden with new murals, furniture, calligraphy and paintings of the highest standard. Greys Court is a fascinating combination of the very old and the very recent.

Right above Brunner family life at Greys Court, as depicted by Lady Brunner's brother, Laurence Irving

Right below The *Country Life* advertisement for Greys Court

Sir Felix Brunner (1897–1982)

Sir Felix's great-grandfather was a Swiss Protestant minister who settled in Lancashire in 1832. Much of the older furniture in the house came from Switzerland, to which Sir Felix returned for his honeymoon and many later walking holidays. His grandfather was the 'chemical Croesus' Sir John Brunner, the co-founder of Brunner Mond, which amalgamated to form ICI in 1926. Sir John was not only a successful businessman, but also stood as a Liberal candidate, and was a philanthropist who supported education and workers' rights, including statutory sick pay. He was a powerful ally of Octavia Hill, the founder of the National Trust. Sir Felix was also active in Liberal politics as a councillor, parliamentary candidate and president of the party (in 1962–3). A gentle man, he had been deeply affected by his experiences as an artillery officer in the First World War, and endured Parkinson's disease in his later years.

Above A family deed box

UTH OXFORDSHIRE

S COURT," ROTHERFIELD GREYS.

Standing in the centre of a lovely park, high up in unspoilt country, a few miles from Henley-on-Thames and easy reach of Reading.
The fine old

PERIOD HOUSE.

Square hall, three reception and billiards room, fifteen bed and dressing rooms, two bathrooms.

ALL MODERN CONVENIENCES.

Garages, stabling, farmery, lodge, two cottages, dower house.

Lovely old grounds, park and woodland.

TO BE LET OR SOLD.

WITH ANY AREA UP TO 280 ACRES.

Illustrated particulars, full plate photographs and plan of GORDON PRIOR & GOODWIN, 27–28, Pall Mall, S.W. 1.

Elizabeth, Lady Brunner (1904–2003)

Lady Brunner was the granddaughter of the Victorian actor-manager Sir Henry Irving, mementoes of whose distinguished career can be seen around the house. Her mother had created the roles of *Trilby* in George du Maurier's play of the same name and Mrs Darling in J.M. Barrie's *Peter Pan*. Lady Brunner also trained as an actress, but did not pursue this career after she married Sir Felix in 1926. However, her theatrical training proved useful when she came to present Greys Court to visitors: 'I am thankful to have belonged to a profession in which serving the public comes naturally.' In between bringing up their four sons, running the house and creating a new garden, Lady Brunner found time to become involved in her local Women's Institute. In 1944 she was elected to the WI's national federation, serving as its chairman from 1951 to 1956. She was an energetic advocate of the WI's Denman College, which was founded in 1948 to provide adult education for women living in the countryside. She was also founder chairman of the *Keep Britain Tidy* campaign. Lady Brunner lived to a great age; she remained amusing company and much loved to the last.

Right above **The Drawing Room featured on this Greys Court Christmas card**

Right below **The Greys Court jam label**